The Wealth Reference Guide:
An American Classic

Authored by Hendrith Smith
Foreword by Bria Clark

First Edition Published in August 2012

ISBN   978-1723392573

Dedicated to my family:

Yanira Noelle Daniel
&
my daughter, Chaya.

Foreword:

The Wealth Reference Guide serves as a replacement for any advice you may have missed about handling money and customizing financial achievements. It introduces the convention of seeding the brain to increase your financial knowledge base.

Not to be confused with an overnight cash advance pass, this guide ought to be received as a mental refresher, a familiar echo that inspires, "oh-yeah, I know about this," at the sight of cash hang-ups. Record this information and recall it when appropriate. This practice builds true confidence, embodied when your actions match the words you speak. In the same style, a natural repetition of speaking life into monetary goals is weaved into the dialogue of The Wealth Reference Guide.

Financial empowerment speaks to the motivation between making the best out of your current situation and realizing you deserve better. I reflect on the principles Hendrith mentions surrounding self-actualization. It's during moments of frustration, when an optimistic vision doesn't align with the constraints of the environment, that a person should draw on these wealth creation principles to bridge the gap. It starts with making the choice to implement the recommendations presented to you.

Consider Hendrith's point to choose creation over the comfort of settling. At first take, this can be harsh; but in practice, this can be modeled with a scalable effort. One morning, I rode the red line metro train from Washington, DC into Bethesda, Maryland. Unexpectedly two young men hopped onto the train and yelled, "IT'S SHOWTIME! IT'S SHOWTIME! IT'S TIME TO PUT A SMILE ON YOUR FACE!" Holding everyone's attention, they proceeded to perform a synchronized dance routine. At its completion, the crowd smiled, clapped, and displayed their gratitude in the form of dollar bills. Those young men offered an uplifting visual performance to an otherwise mundane traveling experience. They didn't walk around begging. They offered something of value which generated financial resources. This is an example of how changing your financial situation begins with changing your mind.

To be accountable to principles within the Wealth Reference Guide you must implement them, regardless to the size of your income. Promotions are often delayed, because the change agent feels they aren't ready for the move. Crippling phrases like, "when I get my stuff together," demonstrate settling into the comfort of delaying opportunity. Decorated here is a poor man's mentality. The Wealth Reference Guide is about training your mind to see through lifestyle traps that block economic advancement. From this temperament, you can create an attitude for abundance. As opposed to forgoing what you desire, carve out a path toward obtainment. Your financial journey may include evaluating whether the products and services incorporated into your lifestyle reflect respectfully on your buying power. Are the decisions you're making working to advance your standard of living?

Creating a mentality for abundance begins with planting seeds. For this reason, I was complemented by Hendrith's request to contribute to the Wealth Reference Guide. This book is dedicated to people who want mental stimulation and practical solutions. Hendrith has organized this read as a reassurance tool, which hammers into the decision-making process. Allow the Wealth Reference Guide to be used in conjunction with your personalized financial plan to affirm your attraction to currency and propel your financial fate

Bria Clark
Financial Advisor

Contents:

A Recognition of Principles

The principles of wealth are true regarding large amounts and small amounts. It all begins with the smallest unit of currency. If all you have is a dollar, invest it with the same care you would invest 100 dollars with, and with repetition your holdings will soon grow to 100 dollars. Then invest that 100 dollars with the same care you would invest 1,000 dollars with, then invest the 1,000 dollars with the same care you would invest 1,000,000 dollars with. Money must be cared for from it's smallest unit, as a child must be cared for from conception. The same way it is important to care for the health of even a fetus still in the womb, it is also important to care for the wealth of even a single dollar.

Proportional and Relative amounts of Money

Regarding money; treat small amounts with the same respect you do/would treat large amounts. Money flows to people who respect it. Treat every dollar like it's related to a Billion.

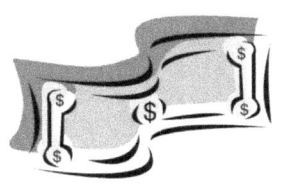

Fear in Relation to Money

If you fear poverty, poverty will come upon you. If you fear wealth, wealth will evade you. Fear and money are horrible companions. Infact, fear and money are enemies.

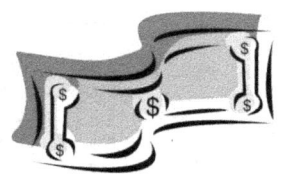

Complaint in Relation to Money

If you complain about the money or resources you lack, you will lack more of it. However, if you are grateful for the money and resources you do have, however small or large it may be, you will gain more of it. Complaint is a cancer to wealth. Gratitude is an amplifier of wealth.

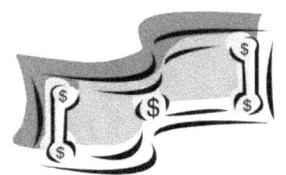

Never Beg

If you beg for money or resources, more begging will be increasingly required. Begging exacerbates void and lack. Instead of begging, find some people to provide value to and ensure that they pay you according to the value you provide.

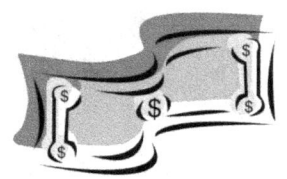

Disorder breeds poverty

Disorder breeds poverty. Anywhere there is disorder, there will also be waste. And waste is one of the many causes poverty. The wise keep their homes and offices neat and clean and organized.

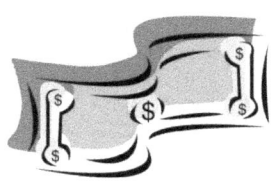

Money is a tool

Money is a tool. As with any tool, it may be used for good or for evil. Therefore, it is important that good people become wealthy so that they have more money to do more good things with.

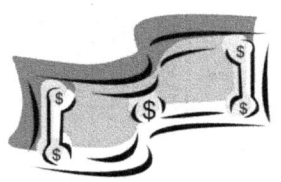

Embracing Capitalism

Having the opportunity to flourish in this Capitalist system of ours, it is important that we help ensure the integrity of the system. We should feed the goose that lays the golden eggs.

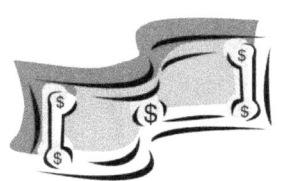

The Nature of Capitalism

In Capitalism, we help ourselves by helping others. Personal gain is achieved through Altruism. Only in Capitalism, is a person required to serve others in order to serve their self. Capitalism is a system of accountability and reciprocity, of mutual benefit and shared prosperity. And it is the system that affords the greatest amount of people the opportunity to afford great wealth while also affording the greatest amount of people the benefit of avoiding severe poverty while also affording great masses of people the luxury of choosing their own financial medium according to their own merit.

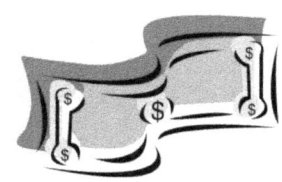

The Social usefulness of money

Don't be motivated by money for it's own sake. Think of all the good things you can do with the money. Think of how much it will benefit your family. And remember that God desires for you to prosper; we were each designed to prosper in our own ways. Since money is the main medium for prospering today, it stands to reason that God would desire you to have plenty of it.

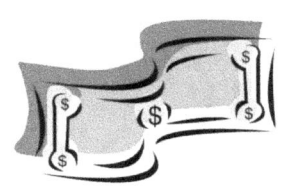

Abundance

Money is abundant. Do not fear that if other people earn more more, the less there will be for you. That's wrong. Because money is like trees and wealth is like forests. It has no conceivable limits, and all lives involved may prosper equally in their own unique way. And the more one prospers, in fact the more potential there is for others to prosper.

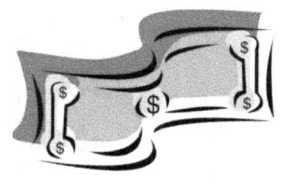

The cure is Capitalism

Poverty would not exist if we had a Capitalist system where everyone involved actively realized their God-given purpose. Each of our wealth is directly correlated to our success at fulfilling our God-given purpose. And just as there is unlimited capacity for collective Human purpose, there is also unlimited capacity for the individual wealth we can enjoy collectively from that. The issue is not whether there is enough wealth to go around - there undoubtedly is more than enough. The issue is whether enough people will reach the level of self actualization required to share in and share of the limitless wealth that exists.

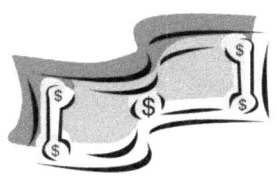

Money Attraction

Money goes where focus goes. We should stay focused on our financial goals. Stay focused on savings and Investments, not on debt. Stay focused on income, not expenses. Stay focused on salary, not bills. Definitely do not ignore the negative (debt, bills, etc) - but give it the minimum attention needed for settlement and resolution. Your focus should be on the direction you desire to go.

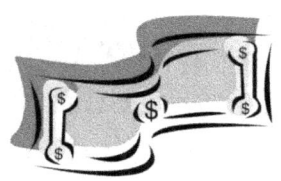

Financial Planning

Just like nature plans out the days and the seasons and measures them in calculated proportions; we should do the same thing with money. Money must be planned for and planned with, and measured into calculated proportions.

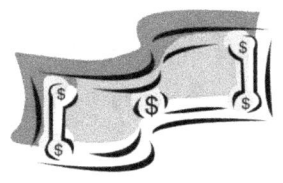

Saving Money

Save like you love your future self,
spend like you honor yourself today.
They way you spend money is
important - never spend money with
fear of lack in mind. Firstly, spend
money only of things and experiences
that provide you superior value.
Spend money knowing that the money
will come right back to you. Have faith
(based on the wisdom of your
spending choice) that the
non-monetary gain you got from what
you spent the money on will help you
to earn more money later in some way.

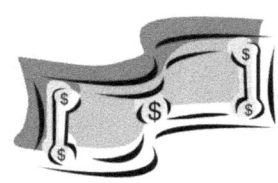

Subconscious Wealth

A persons external Financial reality is the result of whether in their subconscious mind they have wealth consciousness or poverty consciousness. Our consciousness produces spiritual and mental seeds that are planted in our habits and bear fruit in our financial reality.

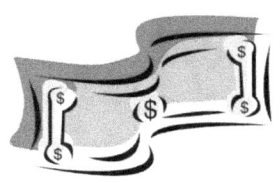

Financial Seasons

We all must endure the Financial seasons of life. Growing wealth is like managing a farm or garden. The wise become good at planting wisely in the fall so they don't have to beg in the spring - And saving and investing in the summer so they don't have to borrow in the winter.

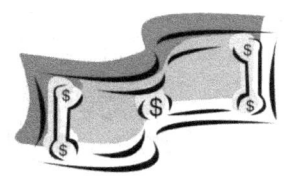

Retention of Money - The Savings Requirement

In order to retain money savings, you must feel in your subconscious mind that you deserve to keep the money. If in your subcontious you feel undeserving, you will always find something to spend the money on or you will attract negative circumstances that require/force you to spend the money. If you calmly feel you deserve to keep the money, you will easily save it and you will be guarded against incoming financial burdens. Be sure that the mind is very powerful and it always gets what it secretly harbors.

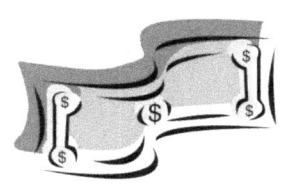

Subconscious roots of Financial Reality

If you are struggling financially, there is definitely a subconscious belief about money that you need to replace with another subcountious belief about money. Change the subconscious belief and eventually your financial situation will also change.

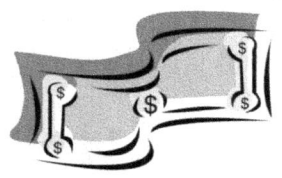

No Handouts

Handouts are like trojan horses that seem nice at first, only to learn later of their fraudulence and how much damage and turmoil and suffering they cause. Instead of seeking a handout, seek a customer. Instead of wanting a handout, find or create a good or service you can sell to some group of people out there who will benefit from it.

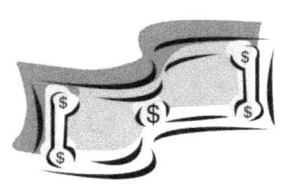

Money Attraction

Money flows where the heart knows money. When you learn the principles of money and wealth and root them in your heart/subconscious mind, you become a magnet for money. that see
It."

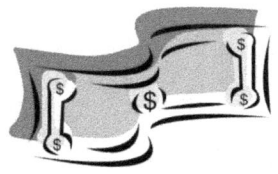

Asset Investments

"I invest in productive assets and not in
unproductive assets. Just like a good
apple
farm produces the most apples (output)
with the least soil, water and sun
(capital/input) needed – a good investment
does the same kind of thing. So the desire
for productive assets is very natural."

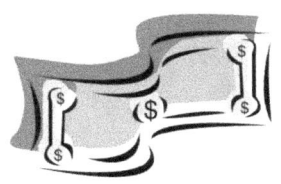

Money is Abundant

Money is abundant. The main question is
'What value can I produce in exchange for
maximum money. What skills, goods, or
services can I sell for the greatest profit.
There is so much money in circulation. There is so much money out
there. Don't worry about
where the money is, or what percent of
people have what percent of the money.
Instead, focus on
producing and providing the skills, good
and services that people are willing to pay
money for.

Self Sufficiency

What a man achieves for himself he will cherish. But what is given to him without exchanged value will be neglected.
Do not go through life looking
for handouts or charity. Do not expect to get anything for
free. Instead – work hard, work smart, and produce value. Because the reward of productivity and personal achievement is a
fulfilling life. And the true cost of receiving handouts is understated.

Note: Charity does so much good and it certainly has it's place. We all receive and give some kind of charity at different points in life. But as with anything, "too much of anything is bad."

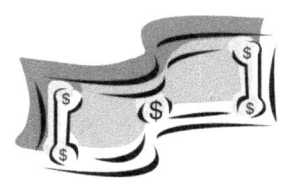

Wealth is proof that a man can command
the cosmos. And poverty is proof he
hasn't mastered the language of nature.
Given that money (and assets) are reward to work well done, and wealth is
an
accumulation of money and assets. hen
wealth is therefore some proof of a ility.
And poverty,
therefore, some proof of lackthereof.

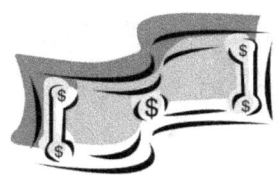

Value Provided

Money earned is proof of value provided. Money earned is proof of worth
recognized.
It is important to have a healthy understanding of what money is.
If you think money is the root of all evil, you will subconsciously
repel money away. But if you understand
that money is a reward to work well done, you will aim to do good work and in return you will expect
and attract money to you.

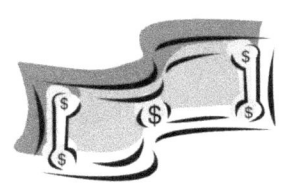

Wealth as it relates to health

In nature, wealth is a prerequisite for health. There is no organism that has health
without first having some wealth. Strive for health, but focus more on wealth.
Some people say they just want to be happy. Some people say that as long as they are
healthy, they will be satisfied. But the reality is that complete health and happiness can only be attained
with having attained some level of wealth. Poverty is an enemy of health. And poverty is an enemy of
happiness. So, seek wealth and aim to use that wealth wisely.

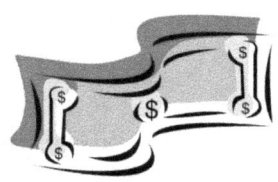

Wealth as it relates to Sustainability

Natures Way is never to waste. The wise
seek out utility and usefulness.
When we look at nature, we
see that the concept of waste does not
exist. Because the
waste of one life is the food or a tool for
another life. So nature is so efficient,
that
everything within it
serves a useful purpose in the ultimate
effort of building wealth and fostering
more
life in nature. In our
personal lives, we should aim to be this
efficient – so that every hour, every
relationship, everything we
own is wisely put to use in the effort of
making our lives better and making
other
people lives better.

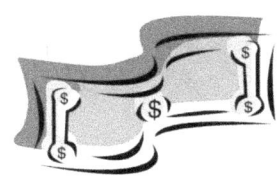

Nature's way is Capitalism

Natures Way is Capitalism – It is always about value given for value earned. It is always about productivity and growth. It is always about utility and usefulness. It is always about Returns on Investment. Nature is the best Capitalist we will ever know. Think about how a forest works, and this will make so much sense. Each of us should take note of this and apply it to our own goal of wealth creation.

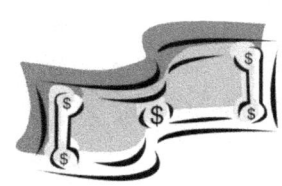

Evolution of our greatest selves

Each of us were designed to live full and
abundant lives. We were designed to maximize our potential
and to continually evolve, just as everything else in nature was designed to
do. Growth and progress is natural. The desire for comfort and wealth
is natural. But mediocrity is not natural.
And The acceptance of poverty is not natural.

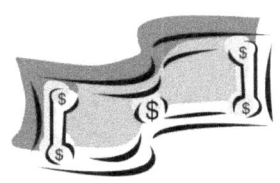

More Life

*When we look at
nature, what we see is life
continually
striving for more life –
mostly through collaboration with
other
lives, and through being of value in
some
way. And as people,
we should be doing the same thing
–*

*seeking more life. And in this day,
money
is the most useful tool for
attaining more life.*

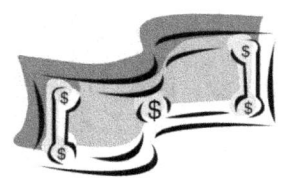

How you speak of money

Vocabulary is important regarding wealth. Assess all of the money related words you use and determine whether you use those words in a faithful way or in a fearful way. Do you speak of Capitalism in terms of opportunity or exploitation? Do you speak of money in terms of the amount you don't have or the amount you do have? Do you speak of business as a bad thing or a good thing? Do you speak of yourself as a victim or a Victor? Do you speak of debts and bills more than you speak of income, savings and Investments? The wise are careful with their vocabulary and the way they speak about money.

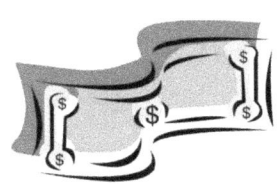

Charity and Brotherly Love

In helping others attain good health; good health is afforded to you. In helping others attain good wealth; good wealth is afforded to you.

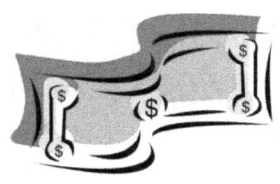

Your Relationship to money

What is your Relationship to money? If you treat money like a good friend who loves your company, it will behave that way. If you treat money like an enemy who aims to destroy you and is always causing trouble, it will behave that way. If you treat money like a stranger who does not know you, it will behave that way. If you treat money like a good parent who knew you from birth and loves you and desires you to prosper, it will behave that way. If you treat money like a slave who works for you but does so unwillingly and will flee at it's first opportunity, it will behave that way. If you treat money like a valued employee who enjoys the work it does for you and does so with excellence and wants to stay with you, it will behave that way. If you treat money like a fling who does not know or love you but only has a temporary lust for you, it will behave that way. If you treat money like a wife or husband who chose you and who you chose and who loves you with profound care and desires to be with you for life, it will behave that way. If you treat money like a prize you do not deserve and are guilty for receiving it, it will behave that way. If you treat money like an award which you worked hard for and deserve to have, it will behave that way.

If you treat money like a name tag that belongs to someone else, it will behave that way. If you treat money like a name tag with your name on it, it will behave that way. If you treat money like a pet who is friendly but lacks intelligence and so must be controlled, it will behave that way. If you treat money like an organically intelligent medium which inherently knows how to best reach fulfilment and only needs your cooperation, it will behave that way. If you treat money like cement which must be made and constructed and propped up and consistently rennovated, it will behave that way. If you treat money like a thriving forest which has in it's dna a natural desire for growth and self expression, it will behave that way. If you treat money like air which one only may keep for a moment and is perpetually dependent to new imputs and outputs, it will behave that way. If you treat money like Earth which is teaming with life and may be farmed and cultivated and replenished and kept and improved upon and used to create more abundance, it will behave that way.

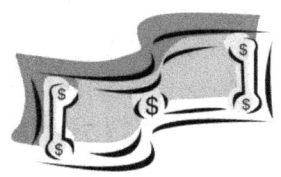

Wealth contiousness

Children are born with wealth contiousness, and had it from before conception, as is true with every life that is conceived and born. But the principles of wealth must be taught to them that they may recall it and retain it and master it in this present life. It begins early, with the first dollars they earn. They must be required to apply the priciples of wealth to the first dollars they earn, and they must be inspired to love the process and the outcomes so that they may continue to lovingly apply the principles of wealth to all future dollars they earn and all future dollars they receive, acquire, or become stewards of.

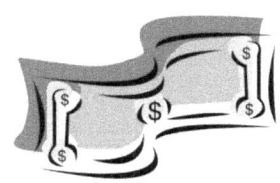

Discussing money with children

Be careful of how you discuss money in front of your children. Never speak of household finances in terms of lack or scarcity in front of your kids. Only speak of household finances in terms of goals and wealth in front of your kids. Your discussions about money will either enrich them with wealth contiousness or cripple them with poverty consciousness. Remember, both you and them and future generations will either benefit from their wealth contiousness or suffer if they have poverty consciousness. Their nature is to prosper, but is matters how you nurture them.

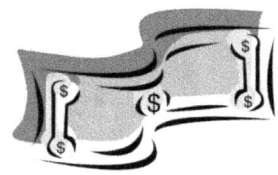

Charitable Contributions

Charity is a vital element to Capitalism. It is charity - the good will and Financial assistance given freely to those that need it by those that have it - that makes it less necessary for government to take the people's money and waste it in a failed effort to do what charity does. Given the fact that government often grows larger in the name of good will efforts and help, Charity helps keeps government limited. And it is necessary that good people perform kind acts for other people.

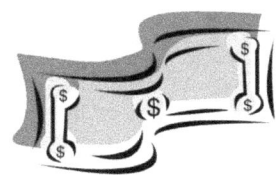

Goal Setting

The person who sees their goal at a distance will never attain it. But the person who feels their goal is already their own will attain it surely and promptly. In the mind, through faith, desired future things may be owned now.

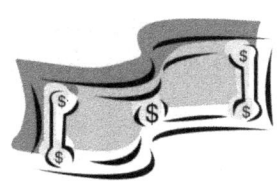

Imagination

Imagination is the engine of creation. As we imagine our goals and desires in our mind, we cause them to become true in our life.

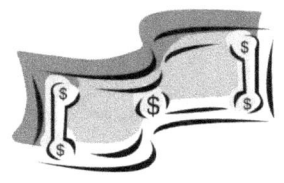

Feeling Wealthy

Feeling wealthy is the beginning of attracting wealth. To attract wealth, you must behave as if you already have the amount of wealth you are expecting.

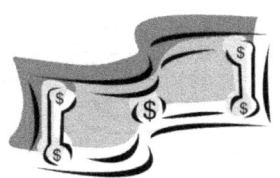

Law of Economic Exchange

There is no such thing as something for nothing. We live in an ordered universe with checks and balances. The law is value earned is according to value provided.

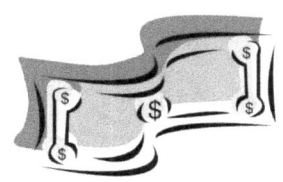

Resourcefulness

The ability to extract maximum value from resources while creating minimum waste - is a profitable skill to have.

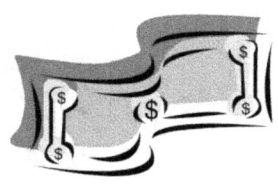

Allocation and Delegation

The ability to allocate resources wisely is a profitable skill.

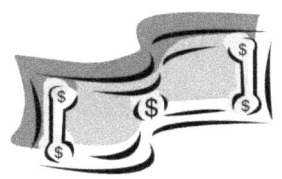

Business

Business is about putting a product or service in the marketplace that will create value for a specific group of people.

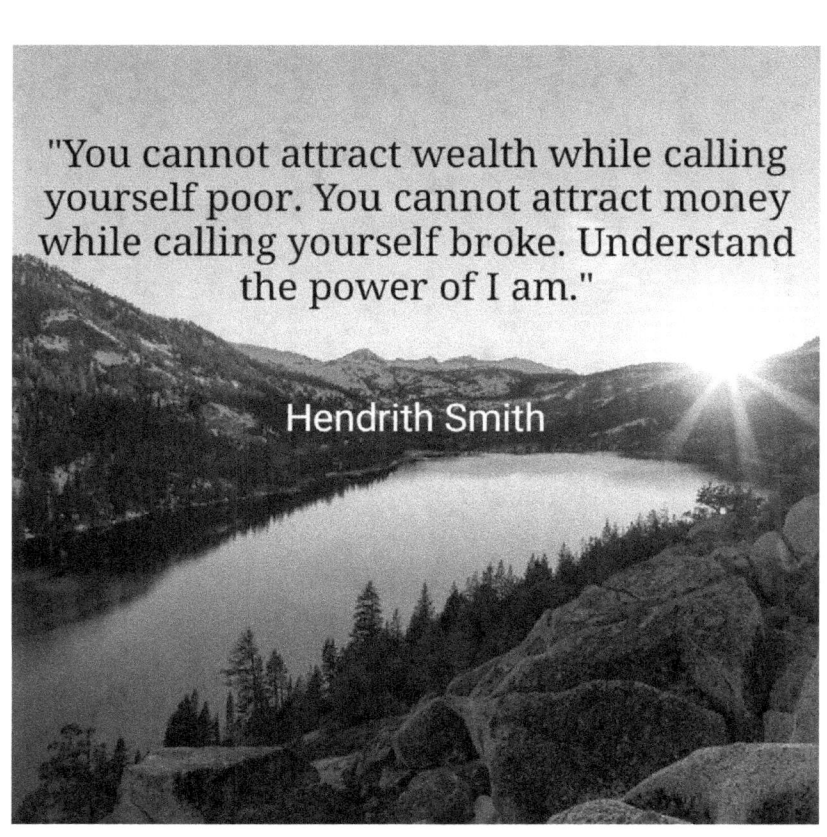

"You cannot attract wealth while calling yourself poor. You cannot attract money while calling yourself broke. Understand the power of I am."

Hendrith Smith

"Money, like the elements of nature - has to always be in action; always moving; always working; always evolving and growing and becoming. This is why wealthy people treat money like it is a living thing - because it is. As alive as the microbes in the soil and the leaves on the trees which through their action and usefulness constitute greater life beyond themselves."

Hendrith Smith
Author of 'The Wealth Reference Guide'

"Dollars are like men. The have to have a purpose for living. And just like men, dollars without purpose quickly degrade themselves or cause destruction. This is why wealthy people give their money meaning and each dollar has a purpose it is working for."

Hendrith Smith
Author of 'The Wealth Reference Guide'

"Part of building wealth is being a good receiver. In the same way that a good cellphone must be able to receive radio waves, a good person must be open to receive wealth. It sometimes comes in the form of money. It sometimes comes in the form of assets, gifts, information, favors, or anything of value."

Hendrith Smith

"With every week that passes, I work to become a better Banker. This is who I am. This is what I do. And I live to be great at it."

Hendrith Smith

"Money is a reward
for work well done."
- Hendrith Smith

"Money earned is proof of value provided."

- Hendrith Smith

"Money earned is proof of worth recognized."

- Hendrith Smith

"Your savings strategy reveals your relationship to life and your relationship to faith and fear. We should save for goals, not emergencies. If you save for a goal, the goal will come to you. If you save for an emergency, the emergency will come to you. Don't be naive enough to ignore the possibility of bad things, but let that come out of your reserve cash-on-hand, not out of some fund specified for crises."

Hendrith Smith

"Everyone has to foster their own version of a healthy relationship with money. While there are certain basic principles to adhere to, a person should also depend on their refined intuition and pure heart regarding their finances. It's a combination of logic and soul."

Hendrith Smith

"Part of the problem of poverty is the poor persons mind. The other part of the problem of poverty is the reality of unchangeable natural laws - once a thing falls below a certain poverty level, the activities of wealth incur a temporary premium while the activities of poverty incur a temporary discount; making it such that wealth incentivises wealth and poverty incentivises poverty. This is because nature values wealth and is designed such that wealth leads to life, and poverty leads to disintegration so that whatever incurred the poverty may be recycled for better use to better ends."

Hendrith Smith
Author of 'The Wealth Reference Guide'

"Money, like the elements of nature - has to always be in action; always moving; always working; always evolving and growing and becoming. This is why wealthy people treat money like it is a living thing - because it is. As alive as the microbes in the soil and the leaves on the trees which through their action and usefulness constitute greater life beyond themselves."

Hendrith Smith
Author of 'The Wealth Reference Guide'

"I am a student of nature. Because nature teaches all of the principles of wealth management, and implements all of the tools of pure Capitalism in a way that no person could ever do better."

Hendrith Smith

"Part of building wealth is being a good receiver. In the same way that a good cellphone must be able to receive radio waves, a good person must be open to receive wealth. It sometimes comes in the form of money. It sometimes comes in the form of assets, gifts, information, favors, or anything of value."

Hendrith Smith

Charity is a vital element to Capitalism. It is the financial assistance given freely to those that need it by those that have it, that makes it less necessary for government to take the peoples money and waste it. The Goodwill of citizens and private charities will always be superior to government programs.

- Hendrith Smith

"Life is war."

Hendrith Smith

"If a person is poor but desires wealth, you may discuss money with them without negative consequence. And in fact you will be blessed to share your wealth consciousness with them. This is a win-win. But if a person is poor but identifies with their poverty, any discussion of money you have with them will result in their poverty being ascribed to you while still retained with them. This is a lose-lose. This is why the wealthy avoid the poor - unless they are desirous of wealth - because poverty by default is a contagious disease of the mind."

Hendrith Smith

"The self-reliance of the Capitalist, should always be tempered by the recognition that our lives are intertwined and there is an inter-dependency between us all that necessitates cooperation for it all to work."

Hendrith Smith